Honey & Pearls

(A Unique Collection Of 100 Word Poems)

ISBN-13:978-1546762379
ISBN-10: 154676237X

All Rights Reserved
L.A.Jones©2017

For

Jamie

Contents

Goodbye
The Noise
Spring
Raindrops
Surf's Up
Space
Soaring
Earth Song
Baby Blues
Winter
Riding High
Swan Lake
Eye Of The Storm
Rocky Ascent
Pickled Palette
Humming Bird Blue
Autumn
Skin Deep
A Shakespearian Odyssey
Bloodied War
Affairs Of The Heart
Honey & Pearls
Sunrise
Blackened Soil
The Selective Jamboree
A Dog's Life
Growing Old Disgracefully
An Artist's Perspective
Summer
Memories

Unforgettable
Footsteps
Serendipity
Driftwood
Pebble Dash
Made Up
Unravelling The Cuckoo
Sanctuary
New York
Origins
Distant Shores
Explorer's Tale
The Struggle
Love
A Soldier's Psalm
Addicted
New Perspective
Cosmetically Correct
India
Keeping Up With The Joneses
Songbird
Edible Youth
Chasing Rainbows
Monkey Business
Grandchildren
Runaway Bride
Row Your Boat
Déjà Vu
Alaska
Happy Feet
Into The Deep
Land Of Make Believe
Fallen Angels
The Sky At Night
Reaper
Unconscious
Roll Up Roll Up
A Squirrel's Song
Ode Of The Smitten
A Parody Of Summer
Singing In The Rain

Hail Caesar
Let There Be Hope
Fated
Perception
Shipwrecked
Grandma's Apple Pie
Jolly Roger
Optical Illusions
The Witching Hour
Take Me To Church
Enlightenment
Capturing Canada
The Ark
Birdsong
Sweet Tooth
Missing In Action
The Life Of Henry The VIII
Broken
Unique
Letting Go
Cheating Heart
Under The Weather
The Two Faces Of Nature
Stand And Deliver
Once Upon A Dream
Have You Ever?
Haunted
My Jamie
It's A Boy Thing

Goodbye

The Babbling Brook
A Hypnotic Sound
Reminding Me Of Happy Times
Paddling On Summer Days
Bare feet
Laughter-
I See Your Beautiful Smile
Through The Hazy Sun
Taking My Breath Away
Lying In The Meadow
Watching The Sky
The Sun
Warming Our Skin
I remember It
Like Yesterday
I Close My Eyes
I Sigh
It's Time…
Carefully
I Remove The Lid
Tears Salt My Cheeks
'Goodbye My Love
Run Free
Fly High'
The Essence Of You
Caught On The Breeze
Swirling Over
The Babbling Brook
I Dip My Toes
The Water Is Cool
I Hear Your Voice
I Smile

The Noise

What's That Noise?
Can You Hear It Too?
Tap
Tap
Tap
It's Driving Me Mad!
I Can't Think!
Tap
Tap
Tap
A Nightingale Flies
The Cuckoo Cries
Tap
Tap
Tap
A Grain Of Sand
In No-Man's Land
Tap
Tap
Tap
Where Is It Coming From?
What Does It Mean?
The Sea Of Blue
The Field Of Green
No Matter Where
No Matter What
I Can Always Hear It!
My Mother Says
'It's Probably A Mouse
Gathering Nuts
In An Underground House'
She Never Hears It
Never Has
She Looks At Me As If I'm Mad!
Tap
Tap
Tap

Spring

A Dew-Kissed Snowdrop
Soft And White
Shimmering With Beauty
The Blackbird Sings
His Morning Song
A New Day Has Begun
Young Buds Grow
On Barren Trees
A Truly Wonderful Sight
The Forest Green
Lush And Bright
Mother Nature Smiles
Light As A Feather
Clean And Free
Floating On The Breeze
The Morning Haze
Burnt Away
By The Rising Sun
Baby Rabbits
Running Free
Prancing Deer
Bumble Bees
Fragranced Scent
In The Air
Insects Burst Forth
Everywhere
The Velvet Beetle
Deepest Black
A Single Hornet
Woodpecker's Tap
The Tiniest Ant
Food On His Back
Spring Has Arrived
Winter Has Packed

Raindrops

Invigorating
Sensations Of A Hundred Slaps
Each Drop
Colder Than The Last
Let Us Dance In The Rain
Head Tilted Back
Awash-
Pearly Water
Crystal Clear
Running Over Skin
Feeling Fresh
Causing Shivers
Stimulation Overload
Like The Air Of The Glacier
Thin
Crisp-
Runaway Blues
Deep As The Moon
Transparency Opaque
Patchy Fog
Damp And Thick
Faded In The Rain-
A Thunderstorm
Of Loudest Clap
A Force
Unleashing Rain
Stirs Emotion Locked Within
Unwrapping Of The Layers-
Take Me Dancing In The Rain
Teach Me To Live Again
Heavy Dew
My Soul Doth Soak
Release Me From This Pain

Surf's Up

The Crest Of A Wave
A Mighty Sight
Surfers Will Ride
In Sheer Delight
The Salted Air
Awakens The Soul
On The Sun-Kissed Beach-
The Gulls Doth Cry
I Wonder Why
Maybe It's Fate
The Spray Is High
Churned Altogether
Frothy And White
Reminding Me Of Home-
Stay Close To The Curl
Honey And Pearl
Flowing In The Breeze
Ariel Jumps
Crazy Stunts
Ripping At The Peak-
Feeling Free
Flying High
Roaring Sea
Ebbing Tide
Overhead Tripled
Rubber Clad Skin
Call Of The Ocean
Locked Within
Streamlined Board
Short And Long
Crest Of A Wave
Majestic And Strong

Space

Astronauts In Orbit
Exploring Outer Space
Seeking Alien Lifeform
In Another Place

Solar System Milky Way
Galactic Galaxy
Asteroid Shower Falling Stars
Cosmic Energy

Infinite Dimensions
Planets Sun And Moon
Endless Possibilities
The Mind Becomes Immune

Quantum Physics Speed Of Light
Still So Much To Learn
Sprightly Comets Burning Bright
Astronomers Who Yearn

A Metallic Iron Meteorite
Crashing To The Ground
Burning Through The Ozone Layer
Debris All Around

Tiny Rings Of Saturn
Nine Moons Around Its Core
Second Largest Planet
One I Most Adore

Lost In Space Call NASA
Black Hole We Fell
Abandoned Forever
Time Will Tell…

Soaring

Wind On My Face
Blowing My Hair
Snow Capped Mountains
Underfoot-
Gliding High
Caught On A Rift
Wisp Of Cloud
Crimson Sun-
Reflections In A Blue Lagoon
Cool And Deep
Midnight Moon-
Lightening Storm
Crackling Bright
Thrum Of Thunder
Dangerous Flight-
Horizon Of Green
Fresh And Clear
Glade Of Shadows
Herd Of Deer-
Swollen Rivers
Salmon Spawn
Serenity Of Dawn's First Light
Seductive Sands Sun-Kissed Beach
Statuesque Alluring-
Man-Made Land
Bronze And Gold
Patchwork Quilt
Fruitful Earth-
Blizzards Rage
Ravine Of White
Newly Fallen Snow-
Misty Fog
Thick And Wet
Blanket Of Disguise-
Soaring Free
Soaring High
Soaring Forever

Earth Song

Stop The Senseless Killing
There Will Be Nothing Left
Irreversible Extinction
Animals Bereft

The Short Sighted Rhino
Nurturing And Free
Numbers At An All Time Low
Killed For Ivory

Breathtaking Big Cats
Amazing Coats Of Beauty
Fashion Trend Painful End
Fur Trade Cruelty

Global Warming Toxic Fumes
Smothering Our Planet
Ozone Layer Danger Looms
Unpredictable Climate

Flash Floods Tsunamis
Snow In June
Land Slides Earthquakes
Life Lost Boom

We Must Take Action
Before It Is Too Late
If We Stand Together
We Can Change Our Fate

Reduce Our Carbon Footprint
Recycle And Reuse
Protecting Generations
Do *Not* Abuse

Baby Blues

Talcum Powder
Cloud Of White
Sudocrem And Suds
Bathtub Antics
Floating Ducks
Slippy Floors And Hugs
The Smell Of Your Skin
Fresh And Light
Your Little Nose Crinkles
In The Moonlight
Ten Perfect Fingers
Ten Fat Toes
A Cute Little Dimple
A Small Button Nose
Like A Rainbow On A Rainy Day
You Light Up My Life
In Every Way
We Have A Routine
It's The Same Every Night
I Sing You A Song
You Gurgle Along
Drink Up Your Milk
Pearly And White
Your Eyes Become Heavy
Your Breathing Light
I Wonder What
You Will Dream Tonight…

Winter

Hardened Earth Barren Trees
Uncaring And Unyielding
Crackled Ice Crystallised
Temperature Is Freezing

Bleak And White Crisp And Fresh
Frosty Plains Clouded Breath
Withered Hands Dry Cracked Lips
Runny Nose Unseemly Slips

Tiny Robin Breast Of Red
Backdrop Blackened Sky
Angelic Pure Perfection
Easy On The Eye

Intricate Falling Snowflakes
Ice Kissed Air
A Panoramic Paradise
Velvet Winter Hare

Grey Washed Peaks Ruffled Cloud
A Monochrome Display
Russet Tones Disappear
Blanket Covered Spray

Whipped Powdered Particles
Floating On The Breeze
Shining In The Moonlight
Artic Freeze

Whiter Than the Lily
Scenery Sublime
Pictures On A Postcard
Frozen In Time

Riding High

The Dusty Paddock
Orchard Bloom
Grey Dappled Mare
Grazing On the Pasture Green
In The Morning Air

Chestnut Gelding
Yonder Field
Golden Rustic Mane
Flexing Muscle Sleek and Lean
Rolling In The Rain

Black Lonely Stallion
Standing On The Hill
Majestic
Magnificent
Very Strong Willed

Contrasting Plains
Another Range
Dartmoor Ponies Dwell
Hardy With A Thick Set Build
Chocolate Caramels

The Shire Horse
A Working Breed
Pulling On The Plough
Gentle Giant Melting Hearts
My Favourite Up Till Now

Let's Not Forget
The Smallest Breed
The Shetland Loved By All
Standing In The Meadow
Only Three Foot Tall

Swan Lake

They Pair For Life
Majestic And White
Reflections On The Moonlit Lake
Ripples Cascading-
Necks Entwined
Slender And Long
Proud Supreme And Noble-
Fair Yonder Maiden
Graceful And Sweet
Dreaming Of A Distant Grace
Yearning
For Love's First Kiss-
Creamy Pale On Waters Blue
Serenity Of Peace
A Sacred Sight
Distant Shores
Tranquility Release-
Ruffled Feathers
Beating Wings
Call Of The Wild
Fierce Protector
Firm And Strong
Always By Your Side-
Blackened Necks
Sleek And True
Set Against The Pale-
Set Me Free
Heart Most True
Stillness Of The Night
Effortless Gliding
Water Break
Neath
Dawn's First Light

Eye Of The Storm

Furious Destructive Force
Heart Of A Lion
Tropical Storm That Started Small
Fully Unleashed Undying

Wildest Wind Deafening Sound
Expanding Terrible Rage
Devastating Thundercloud
Normality Betrayed

Uprooting Homes Trees And Cars
Blown Around Like Paper
Deadly Power Most Severe
Angry Mother Nature

Threatening Sky Grey and Black
Choking Flying Dust
Driving Rain Thrashing Wild
Violent And Robust

Tidal Waves Ten Foot High
Crashing To The Shore
Civilisation Washed Away
Flood Defenses Floored

Tremendous Infernal
Electric Forked Splits
Intensity Quadrupled
Catastrophic Pit

An Unrelenting Surge Most Strong
Uncaring Wild And Free
Changing Direction
Heading Out To Sea

Rocky Ascent

Stunning Rocky Mountains
Rugged Rustic Peaks
Cloud Hidden Summit
Totally Unique-
Upward Climb
Most Challenging
Tired Muscles Ache
Technical Footwork
Crested Hill Break-
Vertical Inclination
Craggy Jagged Stone
Altitude Perspiration
Climber's Free Zone-
Topping Out
Rappel Off
Culminating Goal
Accomplished Perseverance
Dedicated Soul-
Ascending Through The Clotted Clouds
Coolness On My Face
Demanding Pitted Stony Ground
Arduous Embrace-
Reddened Hands Tired Feet
Windswept Grace
One Last Push To Finish Strong
Precipitous Pace-
Such A Euphoric Feeling
Standing At the Top
Himalaya's Conquered
This Expedition Clocked-
Thrills And Jubilation
Mountaineering Dreams
Another Chapter Overcome
Live Life To The Extreme!

Pickled Palette

Popsicles And Oysters
Stuff That Doesn't Go
Jumbled Altogether
Green Tomatoes
Peanut Butter
Dunked In Tea
Lemon Meringue Pie
Chocolate Balls
Soaked In Brine
Banoffee Ice-Cream Fries
Wobbly Jelly
Heinz Baked Beans
Served Upon A Plate
Sausages
Clotted Cream
Deep Fried Dates
Anchovies And Pancakes
Strawberries And Mash
Fish Pie Milkshake
Corned Beef Hash
Bread And Butter Pudding
Soaked In Vindaloo
Drizzled With A Hint of Gin
Hot Dog Stew
Eggy Bread And Chopsticks
On A Rainy Day
Profiteroles
Mayonnaise
Crème Brûlée
All Of Which Are Lovely
If Eaten On Their Own
Put Them Altogether
Take Me Home!

Humming Bird Blue

Tiniest Form Of Beauty
'Tis Beating On The Wing
Tinted Blues Upon The Light
Hues Of Bottled Green-
Iridescent Feathers
Hovering Figure Of Eight
Ruby Breasted Treasure
Dainty Delicate-
Seeking Nectar Sweetest
Pure As Golden Sun
Tapered Bill Of Inky Black
Subtle Undertones-
A Compact Hearty Warrior
Visual Displays
Extremely Territorial
Contrasting Light And Shade-
Blue-Tailed Emerald
Fiery Topaz
White Tuffed Sunbeam
Breeds With A Pizzazz-
Fascinating Creatures
Fairy-Like To Watch
Mesmerising Antics
Smooth As Butterscotch-
Creamy Textured Tufty Plume
Vibrant Shimmered Light
Biggest Heart Incredibly Smart
Rapid Moving Flight-
Amazingly Versatile
Beautiful Free
Unique Uplifting
Tranquility

Autumn

Richened Hue Upon The Air
Warmth Of Summer Fading
Golden Yellows
Copper Browns
Continuous Cascading-
Caught Upon A Simple Breeze
Floating Down To Earth
Rusted Leaf
Foregone Fruits
Laid Around The Girth-
Crunch Of Autumn Underfoot
Bronzed Horizon
Mellow Haze
Rainy Days
Perpetual Landscape Lies In-
Farmer's Harvest Field Of Gold
Offering Most Fruitful
Celebration
Thankfulness
Coloured Tone Neutrals-
'Twere A Cloud In Autumn
Fluffed Peak Brushed Aside
Textured
Formation
Changing Like The Tide-
Crocus Perennial Flower
Blooming In The Meadow
Milky Cream
Softened Sheen
Variety Of Yellow-
Festival Of Fashion
Season Of Change
Invigorating
Freshness
Barren Home Range

Skin Deep

Hardened Blackwood
Olive Shade
Eclipse Of The Moon-
Darkened Richness
Cool And Deep
Raven Inky Tone-
Smooth And Milky
Creamy Pale
Softest Flake Of Snow-
Lily Fair
Lightest Cloud
Alabaster Beaux-
Warmest Copper
Coral Bronze
Harvest Chocolate Moon-
Autumn Leaf
Fired Clay
Russet Orange Dune-
Dusky Pink
Blushing Hint
Rose Blossomed Hue-
Cameo Sheen
Coral Sand
Cotton Candy View-
Black Or White
Rose Or Brown
Saturated Skin-
Colour Does Not Define Us
It's What Comes From Within-
No Prejudice
No Racism
No Cultural Divide-
Peaceful Harmony
Loving Heart
Discrimination Gone-
Equal Kindness Shown To All
No Coexistent Qualms

A Shakespearian Odyssey

Yonder Range
Youthful Rasp
Thorough Bush
Thorough Branch
Over Peaks
Over Pail
Thorough Storm
Thorough Sail
Lest I Roam Free
Soft And Light
Gilded Flight
Regal Fight
Ye Must Serve
A Righteous King
Clave Of Knights
Hardened Steel
He Bequeath
Transparent Queen
Milder Seas
Waves Of Green
Cloud Of White
Golden Sun Shining Bright
A Yonder Saviour
Thee Whom Seeks
Poppy Red
Brightened Peak
Thee Doth Glow
'Twere Pearly Jewel
Angelic Lair
Reflective Moon
Revolving Dream
Would Tears I Cry
Maiden Fair
The Twisted Blade Cuts Deep
Nourished Qualms
A Hallowed Earth
Sonnet Of A Lowly Poet

Bloodied War

The Sounded Sirens
Ringing Fierce
Oh Panic Stricken Foe
Ravishing Deliverance
Scarcely Touching Souls-
The Oily Bombs
Black As Death
Choking Bloodied Wrath
Labour's Lost
A Mindless Deed
Blinding Murky Blast-
Limbs Stripped Bare
On Fertile Earth
Claret Thickened Soil
Coldest Steel
Recoiled Breeze
Bearing Fruitless Toil-
Misery Inflicted
Innocent Blood Is Shed
Spilling Forth
A Scarlet Stream
Richest Ruby Bled-
Muddied Sinking Trenches
Clogged With Thickest Clay
The Stench Of Desperation
Enemy Hath Slayed-
Reaper Scythe Most Hardy
Awaiting Soldier Blue
Only A Handful Of Plenty
Escape Its Wrathful Rule-
War Is Blind
So Unkind
Conflicted
Bleakest
Black

Affairs Of The Heart

Wandering Lust A Roving Eye
'Tis A Dangerous Game
Heart Is Loving Extra Time
Midst Of Rolling Hay
Romancing Danger Heats The Vein
Excitement Multiplied
Grass Seems Much More Greener
On The Other Side
Euphoric Trist Of Bluest Dream
Upon The Rising Moon
Captured In A Heated Fling
Ashen Fated Doom
No Sooner Than It Started
The Lust Begins To Fade
Crushing Dreams A Plenty
Innocence Portrayed
Tears Flowing Frequently
Pain That Is Achieved
The Future Marred
Think Long And Hard
Fingers Burnt
Reality Learned
The Highest Price Is Paid
In The Coldest Light Of Day

Honey & Pearls

Sickly Sweet Of Nectar Bloom
Humming On The Wing
Waxen Combs Of Honey Gold
Purest Yellow Pale

Oyster's Fruit In Ocean Blue
Single Milky Pearl
Precious Bead Of Elegance
Creamy Jewel Unfurled

Thickest Drop Of Sheer Delight
Oozing Yellow Warmth
Delicious And Unrefined
Nectar Reformed

Elegance Most Blinding
A Timeless Display
All Perfectly Cultured
In Every Way

Sticky Tempting Goodness
Sustaining And Divine
Fragranced Aroma
Sumptuous And Fine

Highest Of Society
Adorned In Jewels Most Pure
Sophisticated Quality
Polished Pearl Demure

Combined Contrasting Elements
Silk Pearl Warmest Honey
An Extravagance Of Elegance
Gold Fair Orb Most Sunny

Sunrise

'Tis Like The Crowning
Anticipated Delight
The Birth Of Jubilation
Emotion Rising High

'Tis Like The Chorus
Melody Divine
The Ol' Blackbird Heralds
As Dawn Awakens Thy

'Tis Like The Mission
Awe Inspiring Fate
A Rocket Leaves Earth's Orbit
The Chilling Moon Awaits

'Tis Like The Chapter
Turning A New Leaf
Joyful Apprehension
Imagination Unleashed

'Tis Like The Tasting
Tastebud Overload
Patience Is Rewarded
A Delicious Meal Is Cooked

'Tis Like The Finding
Of Money In Ol' Jeans
Brightening An Afternoon
Euphoric Spending Dream

Sunrise Is The Beginning
Of A Brand New Day
Where Anything Is Possible
Awakened Namaste

Blackened Soil

Harvest Plough
Turning Soil
Marred Blackened Earth
Tinted Hue
Fruitless Reap
Yonder Field Of Blue-
Toxic Spill
Poisoned Peat
Boggy Doom
Appearance Bleak
Eco-System Challenged
Filtration Peaked-
Darkest Rich
Between The Thumb
Cast Out Resolute
Moistened Web
Pitchest Black
Ashen Charcoal Heap-
Grinding Dirt
Raw And True
Sifted Through The Sheaf
Silted Soil Replenished
Chemical Relief-
Seeds Are Sown A Plenty
Bare On Muddied Earth
Covered Velvet Richness
Wholesome New Birth-
Impregnating Life Again
The Seeds Begin To Grow
Harvest Is Bountiful
Ripe Laboured Toil-
Sensational Sustaining
A Brand New Birth
Delectable Delightful
Death Has Been Reversed

The Selective Jamboree

Absence Makes A Stronger Heart
That Is What They Say
Yesterday Is History
Tomorrow A Day Away

Wrap Me Up In Cotton Wool
Keep Me Safe From Harm
Deliver Me From Evil
Fill Me With Your Charm

A Wise Old Owl Once Told Me
To Always Be Myself
For Everyone Else Is Taken
I Now Know What He Meant

So Many Books So Little Time
Experience The New
Filling Up On Knowledge
'The Taming Of The Shrew'

So Play For Me A Melody
A One That Is Unique
But Others Will Be Jealous
So Turn The Other Cheek

A Dog's Life

Scratchy Sniffy
Loppy Dog
Always Has An Itch
Visits Every Lamp Post
Digs In Every Ditch-
Muddy Prints
On Whitest Floor
Rolling In Manure
Chewing Shoes
Slobber Clues
Things One Must Endure-
Invading Of The Dustbin
My Doggies Favourite Trick
Sneaking On The Bed At Night
Woken By Wet Licks-
Howling Over Emmerdale
Stealing The Best Seat
Panting In One's Ear Lobe
Really Is Unique-
Regardless Of His Misfortunes
He's A Faithful Pet
One That Would
Lay Down His Life
Worthy Of Respect-
My Buddy
My Protector
My Listener
My Rock
Floppy Eared Fuzzball
Wet Nosed Locks

Growing Old Disgracefully

I Have The Mind Of A Younger Soul
Footloose And Carefree
And I Always Bring The Fun
To Any Party
I Love To Travel Far And Wide
Discovering New Things
Meeting People Everywhere
Earning My New Wings
Now My Youth Is Fading
As I Turn Ninety-Three
My Spirit Tries To Escape
This Clapped Out Old Body
Sneaking In The Moonshine
Causing Quite A Stir
Running Rings Around The Staff
Of Which I Must Concur
Alas That Will Never Phase Me
I'm Stubborn To The End
Tearing Up This Rest Home
When Will It Ever End

(Live Life!)

An Artist's Perspective

The Mind Is Like A Prism
Held Captive
Imagination
Ideas Float
Bouncing
Vetted Isolation-
Tunnel Vision Focus
A One Track Mind
Touching Paint To Canvas
Thoughts Become Alive-
Exploding Into Action
Colours Bright And Free
Reminding Me Of India
Traditional Holi-
Moulding With My Fingers
Tweaking With My Brush
Shaping With My Mind's Eye
Becoming With My Touch-
Extraordinary Concepts
Jumping From The Frame
Causing An Emotion
Remembering A Dream-
The Best Is A Reaction
Different Every Time
Laughter
Tears
Anger
Utterly Sublime-
An Artist's True Ambition
Sharing Of His Dreams
Changing Ways Of Thinking
Liberated
Free

Summer

Temperatures Are Soaring
Over Forty Degrees
The Smell Of Pasted Sunscreen
On The Faintest Breeze
The Ground Is Cracked And Blistered
The Unrelenting Sun
Bleaching Of The Landscape
Summer Has Begun
Paddling Pools And Sun Hats
Lots Of Garden Fun
Water Guns Soggy Shorts
Run Rabbit Run
Arriving At The Seaside
Ebbing Of The Tide
Sandy Picnic Sandwiches
Castles Swept Aside
Paddling By The Water's Edge
Swimming In The Sea
Burying The Feet Of Babes
Giggling With Glee
Bronzed Burnt Skin
Panting Dogs
Searching For The Shade
Barbecues Are Active
Sizzling Burgers Round
Strawberries And Ice Cream
Outdoors Sounds

Memories

Although Your Presence May Be Gone
Your Spirit Lingers On
Even If The Scent Of You
Is Now Faded And Gone

I Remember You With Pictures
A Captured Time Stood Still
Experiencing Our Happy Times
Laughter Is The Pill

Closed Eyes For Just A Moment
It Feels Like You're Still There
You Live On Through Our Children
Your Essence Is Flowing There

Sometimes A Little Mannerism
Reminds Me Much Of You
Your Quirky Imperfections
My Fondness For You Grew

I Feel Your Presence Around Me
Hugging Me So Tight
It Gives Me Total Confidence
To Carry On With Life

Unforgettable

Sometimes I Think
That I See
Someone That Is
Lost To Me
I Catch A Glimpse
Or Smell A Scent
A Fleeting Glance
Of Memories Spent
I Wonder How
You Would Be
Ten Years Older
Taller Than Me
Your Soft Brown Eyes
Your Dimpled Chin
Wise Beyond Your Years
Although This Earth
You No Longer Walk
In The Flesh And Bone
Your Spirit Remains
It's Most Sincere
I Feel It More At Home
That Unseen Image
In The Corner Of My Eye
Always Beside Me
I Wonder Why
My Darling Boy
Until I Die
I Will Always Love You

Footsteps

The Softest Crunch Of Fallen Snow
Muffled Underfoot
Imprinted On The Whitest Layer
Softest Flakes Afloat

The Snapping Of A Crackled Twig
Crushed Beneath The Weight
The Smell Of Forest In The Air
Crunching Wood In Haste

The Softest Grain Of Golden Sand
Between The Barefoot Toes
Golden Warm Rich Autumn Hue
Romantic Undertones

Embers Burning Fiery Glow
Orange Heated Mass
Mind Over Matter
Walking Steady Fast

Muddy Prints In Boggy Fields
Thick And Choking Soil
Squelching Sink With Every Step
Quite A Grinding Toil

Slippy Prints On Marble Floor
Leading From The Tub
Evaporation
Rub A Dub Dub

Serendipity

Hidden Forest
Mystic falls
Kaleidoscope Of Dreams
Tucked Away
Beneath A Veil
Blanketed Supreme

A Slice Of Heaven
Is Revealed
Balanced Urban Dream
A Stunning Beauty
Stowed Away
Bursting At The Seams

The Aroma Of Sweet Nature
Wrapped Around The Pores
Enhances Equilibrium
Stimulates The Soul
A Spectrum Of Colour
Neutrals Cloaked In Bold

A Wonderful Discovery
Stunning Sight Most Rare
The Mountain Gorilla
Silver Upon His Back
Majestic And Intelligent
Fur Of Softest Black

I Never Want This Leave This Place
Temptations Call To Me
A Pathway To Perfection
Primary Display
Realm Of Sensitivity
Nature Wild And Free

Driftwood

Floating On The Water's Edge
Ebbing On The Tide
Washed Up On The Shoreline
Marine Debris Doth Glide

Providing Shelter And Food For Birds
Fish And Other Aquatics
Ashen Coloured Floating Wood
Dead Bark Flooded Forest

Becoming The Foundation
For Sand Dunes On A Beach
Transformation Of The Wreckage
Into Something Quite Unique

Decomposing Gribbles
Providing Nutrients
Released Into The Food Web
Nature's Hidden Talent

Lost Cargo Or Shipwrecks
Consumed Within The Sea
Transformed Into Driftwood
A Soft Tranquility

In Norse Mythology Legend
Of Drifting Ash And Elm
It Created Ask And Embla
Where The God Of Odin Dwelt

Pebble Dash

Pitted Pebble On The Beach
Cloaked In Mystery
Where Did You Come From
Washed Up On Bluest Sea

Variety Of Colours
Range Of Size And Shapes
Sometimes Smooth And Shiny
Sometimes Rough And Grey

I Wonder How Long You've Been Here
Present On This Earth
I Wonder If A Dinosaur
Has Walked Over Your Girth

You Are A Fascination
A Wonderment Of Awe
A Beautiful Creation
Even With Your Flaws

Placed Into My Pocket
My Piece Of History
Light Enough To Carry
A Pure Simplicity

Oh Perfect Pebble
From The Sea
Will Always Be
So Special To Me

Made Up

A Flush Of Pink
The Apple Swirled
Brushed Lightly On The Skin
Complexion Fair
Flawless-
Brightest Red
A Statement Bold
Painted Ruby Lips
Puckered
Sensual
Loving Dusted Kiss-
Smokey Eye
Silver Grey
Lined With Darkest Flick
Blended Tones
Softened Shade
Lashes Long And Thick-
Reflective Light
Highlighter Sheen
Set Against The Shade
Adding Depth
Texture Built
Giving Lift And Shape-
Feeling Great
Looking Good
Confidence Displayed
Fresh Cool
Lightest Mood-
The Smallest Hint Of Colour
The Brightest Tint Of Lips
Rosy Glow
Flawless Skin
Transformation Fixed-
Flowing Sun-Kissed Summer
Warming Youthful Peak
Alive And Bright
Beauty So Unique

Unravelling The Cuckoo

I Am A Pretty Feathered Fiend
A Medium Sized Bird
Blue And Grey Upper Plumes
White Under Wing
A Sleek And Shiny Body
Long Tail Pointed Wings
Similar To A Sparrowhawk
Or A Collared Dove
A Fascinating Species
Brown When We Are Young
We Are A Summer Visitor
A Well Known Brooding Cheat
Females Lay Their Eggs In Nests
Which Are Not Their Own
Duping The Unsuspecting Host
Parenting Skills Unknown
Fond Of Hairy Caterpillars
And Other Insects Too
I Am A Folk Song
A Russian Film
A Novel
And A Clock
A Diversity Intensified
Madness Unlocked

Sanctuary

Floating Slowly
Golden Pond
Clear Water Still
Fingers Dip
Lightest Touch
Cooling Silky Skin
Rippled Water
Clear Blue Sky
Sunny Afternoon
Meadow Blossom
Pastel Shade
Healing Vision True
Velvet Flower
Pasture Green
Translucent Dragonfly
Speckled Flush
Harmonic Flow
Satin Spill
Warmest Field
Of Poppy Red
Set Against The Wheat
Dreamy Picturesque Display
Beautiful Retreat
Restoration Of The Soul
The Vibrant Calm Unique
Folding Of The Seasons
A Timeless Classic Feel
The Effortless Utopia
Captivates The Heart
Collective Jubilation
Milestones Apart
My Perfect Haven
Nestled By The Sea
Cloaked In Supremacy
Nowhere Else
On This Earth
Would I Rather Be

New York

The Oily Slick Of City Life
Skyscrapers Tall And High
The Buzzing Thrall Of Chaos
A Cloaked Smokescreen So Dry

Stripy Suits And Heightened Dreams
The City That Never Sleeps
Iconic Hand Of Freedom
Overlooks The Streets

A Snobbery of Classes
A World Of Extreme Wealth
The Luxury Condos
Is Money Well Spent

Designer Shops And Handbags
Fifth Avenue And Third
Guggi Fashion Clientele
Chic Expense Absurd

Bagel Stands And Hotdogs
Traditional Yellow Cabs
Theatre Shows On Broadway
Musicals Most Grand

The Vast Expanse Of Central Park
Is Nestled Deep Within
A Stunning Green Haven
Popular Tourist Dream

Origins

Your Love Unconditional
An Innocence Foretold
Protective Arms That Hold You
Sheltering The Blow

The Ability To Nurture
Powerful And Whole
Parents Leave A Footprint
Like Rings Around The Soul

Always There Through Testing Times
Your Corner They Will Fight
Proud Of Your Achievements
They Are Your Shining Light

High Moral And Values
Passed Down Throughout The Tree
Branched Pure Perfection
Cloudless Eyes That See

The Gift Of Life You Gave Me
Teaching Right From Wrong
Guiding Me Specifically
My Personality Shone

My Love For You Is Timeless
Like Beauty And The Beast
You Are Everything
Without I'm Incomplete

Distant Shores

The Little Boy That Cried Wolf
One Too Many Times
The Hand Of Time
A Quartz Of Clock
Tick
Tick
Tock
A Cratered Crust Of Whitest Moon
Dimpled Throughout Time
A Sheet Of Steel
The Echoed Pitch
Drip
Drip
Drap
Upon A Bridge Of Olden Stone
The Goats That Came To Cross
Forever On To Pastures New
Of Greenest Luscious Grass
Trip
Trap
Trap
Golden Sands Of Bluest Shore
Hidden Secret Caves
A Stunning Coastline To Enjoy
Kissed By Lapping Waves
Splish
Splash
Splosh
A Tiny Seed To Flourish Fourth
Forests To Explore
Reality Inditement
Always Wanting More

Explorer's Tale

Oh Yay To The Nigh
Ships Passeth By
Laden Down With Loot
Neath The Light
Of Yonder Sun
Voyage Wise And True

Discovery Of Untouched Lands
The Richest Spoils Anew
Chartering The Wildest Seas
Neath The Moon
A Silver Shone
Sailing Sure And True

A Native Clan
With Spears Taut
Unfriendly And Unyielding
A Different Language
Way Of Life
Offerings Appeasing

Hottest Sun
Scorched Burnt Skin
A Paradise Of Beauty
Trading Furs
Coffee Beans
Riches Before Thee

With Many Oceans Sailed And Gone
Discoveries Were Great
A Paradise Of Treasured Wealth
Fortune Dictates
Yonder Golden Shore
Destiny Awaits

The Struggle

Digested Rifts
Remain Unsaid
Words Fail Thee
The Silence Is Unarming
Disproportionate In Rhythm
Stubborn As An Age Old Ass
Last Word Always Said
Opposing Conundrum
Battle Plans Are Drawn
Thin Like The Dialogue
At The Crack Of Dawn
Hopeless Romantic
Put Out To Graze
Folded Arms
Hastened Charms
Rolling Eyes A Raging Storm
The Quiet Is The Struggle
Arming Of The Guard
Forward Pace Unthwarted
Engulfed Within A Force
Single Minded Bigots
Unopened To The Truth
Compromise Unwilling
Crossroad Has Been Reached
Broken Words And Promises
Hollowed Vows
Stripped Bare
Removal Of A Rosy Tint
Different Glare

Love

Heart Is Heavy
Seams Are Fat
Love Has Filled The Soul
The Body Is In Unison
Flowering Its Seed
Shining Jubilation
Crested Like The Breeze-
Spread Broad
Like An Angel's Wing
Delicate And Strong
Harmonies Of Summer
Nights Are Cool And Long-
Refreshing Touch
Caressing Skin
A Lover's Story Told
Inspiring Creation
Love Most Pure
Like Gold-
Leaping Rhythm Of A Beat
Dancing To The Tune
Blinded By The Fire Within
Fuller Than The Moon-
Overwhelming Feeling
Happy And Content
A Rejuvenation
That Is Heaven Sent-
The Two Are One
The One Is Two
Sated Desires
Infatuation
Burning
Fires

A Soldier's Psalm

A Deafening Silence
Across The Land
The Fields Of Poppy
Reddened
The Split Blood Of War
Spread Thick
Gone But *Never Forgotten*
Courageous To The End
So Many Lives Lost
The Muddied Trenches
Stale With The Stench
Death Lingers
Intoxicating
A Choking Hold
Young Men
Turned To Dust
Never To Return Home
We *Remember* You
Always
Your Sacrifice Of Life
Selfless
Monuments With Names Inscribed
Wreath Of Poppy
At Your Side
Standing Proud
Your Country Served
Lest We *Never Forget*
Thankyou
Oh **Thankyou**
You Paid The Highest Price
But Know This
Your Legacy
Will Live On
Forever

Addicted

You Wicked Wrench
With Acid Tongue
Take Back What You Said
No Child Should Witness
Your Demise
They Should Be In Bed

You Need Help
You Are Sick
That Demon In A Bottle
Has Cast His Spell
Upon My Love
Her Family Forgotten

Missed The Signs
You Hid It Well
Noticed It Too Late
My Little Ones
Have Lost Their Mom
You Choose Drink

I Try To Help
To Understand
I Can't Sympathise
You Need An Expert
Who Knows Best
To Have A Chance

Free Yourself
Cast Him Out
This Demon
Let Him Go
Reject Him
Tell Him So

New Perspective

When Did It Happen?
What Does It Mean?
Always Unanswered Questions
Too Busy
Always Too Busy
Wrapped Up With Life
Insignificant Now...
Wasted Woes In A Synthetic World
None Of Which Matters Anymore
How Could It Again?
We Are But A Grain Of Sand
Blowing Around This Planet
It Was Routine
Alas I Nearly Missed It
Life...
Change Is Coming
As Sure As The Seasons Of Time
I Will See The World
This Wonderful World
New Cultures
New People
A Richness Of Experience
Firsthand
I Feel Weightless
Like The Soaring Gull
Over The Ocean Spray
(Free)

Cosmetically Correct

Hint Of Sandlewood
Musky Yet Light
A Ray Of Sunshine
Dawn's First Light
Complexion Of Rose
Hints Of Pink
Seduction On A Whim-
An Earthy Moss
Of Foliage Bright
Fresh And Awakening
Base Most Light
Peppermint Paradise
Soothing And Cool
Foundation Most Appealing-
The Bronzing Glow
Of Sun-Kissed Skin
Palette Of Colour
Aroma Of Sin
The Delicate Balance
For Sensitive Skin
Balanced And Healing-
Loose Lips Sink Ships
Puckered Edge
Cherry Kiss
Satin Sheen
Glossy Sight
Brightest Red
Or Palest White-
Egyptian Cotton
Cool And Crisp
Sensual Satin
A Lover's Kiss
Chocolate Cream
Duck-Egg Blue
Richest Colour Alluring

India

A Populous Democracy
Cultured Land Of Beauty
Exotic Plants Of Vivid Colour
A Rich Diversity
The Smells Of India
Awakening
Aromatic
The People Awe Inspiring
Silky Soft Preened Dress
A Heritage Of Asia
The Best Of The Best
The Elephant And Tiger
Famous To The Region
Stunning Hidden Wildlife
A Truly Famous Legion
The Beauty Of The Lotus
India's National Flower
Unfolded In The Asian Sun
Holy And Empowered
A Symbol Of Enlightenment
Considered True And Free
Vibrant Life Within A Bud
Waiting To Open And Be
The Collective Band Of Cultures
Opinionated Belief
Is What Makes
India Unique

Keeping Up With The Joneses

Freshly Mowed Lawn
Stripy And Green
Neatest Cut Privet
That I've Ever Seen
Uniformed Flowers
In Pots Of Gold
Must Follow Suit Indeed

New Red Shiny Sports Car
Parked In Their Drive
Delivers The Wow Factor
Compared To Our Ride
Their Sofas Imported
From Milan Don't You Know
While Ours Were On Offer
BOGOF As It Goes

I Can Take It Or Leave It
It Doesn't Bother Me
My Wife On The Other Hand
Has To Be Queen
So Out with The Old
And In With The New
We Have To Be Hipper
Than Ninety-Two

Songbird

Sing Me A Song
Oh Little Blue Lark
'Tis Quiet In The Meadow
And Summer Doth Start

Lift Up The Spirits
Sing Us A Tune
That Beautiful Sound
Like Waves On The Moon

Makes One Feel Warm
So Fuzzy Inside
Like Pink Cotton Candy
Fluffy And Wide

Your Wings Are Majestic
Your Body So Sleek
Your Perfect Concerto
Doth Make Me Weep

So Sing Little Songbird
Sing Loud And Free
Your Spirit Enticing
It Captivates Me

For Something So Small
Your Song Can Be Heard
Powerful And Strong
Delicate Bird

Melody Sacred
Nationwide
Grace So Special
Bursting With Pride

Edible Youth

There's Nothing Quite Like It
Freshly Baked Bread
The Aroma Of Goodness
Locked Inside One's Head-
The Iced Finger Bun
Ah That Takes Me Back!
To Youthful Times
Bus Money Spent
The Long Walk Home
At The End Of The Day
Worth Every Second
That Sweet Pastry-
The Hot Steaming Mug
Of Chocolate Melt
Topped With Marshmallows
Is Heaven Sent-
Rainy Days
Stuck Indoors
Painting And Baking
Cakes Of All Sorts-
Ten Penny Chews
At The End Of The Week
Savoured Most Slowly
Sticky And Sweet-
Dampers And Beans
Like My Nan Used To Make
Filling
Wholesome
Deliciousness

Chasing Rainbows

Somewhere Over The Rainbow
On A Rainy Day
The Sun Still Shines
It's Madness
A Rainbow Has Come To Play

A Lucky Little Leprechaun
Cloaked In Emerald Green
Has Buried His Treasure
Under Foot
A Rainbow Chaser's Dream

Red And Palest Yellow
Purple Blue And Green
Not Forgetting Orange Or Pink
Bright Strips Of The Beam

Once Upon A Rainbow
I Dreamt
A Dream Of Dreams
Following The Pot Of Gold
Just Bursting At The Seams

So Play For Me A Miracle
Come Shower Me With Luck
The Arch Of Colour
Peeking Through
The Rainy Haze On Earth

Monkey Business

I Was Born Right Here
Within This Zoo
A Conservation First
All The People Come To Stare
A Controversial Burst-
I Live A Life Of Riley
Playing All Day Long
Annoying Older Siblings
With My Silly Qualms-
My Father Has No Patience
His Silver Back Shows Age
I Never Push My Luck With Him
It Is Not Worth His Rage-
We Have A New Enclosure
Bigger Than The Last
It's Absolutely Wicked
We Always Have A Blast-
I Love My Family Down Time
All Huddled In Our Nest
The Nosy People All Gone Home
It Really Is The Best

Grandchildren

There Is Nothing That Compares To This
The Feeling A Grandchild Brings
A Love That Will Consume You
Your Fingers To Your Toes
A Bursting Heart Filled With Pride
Bringing Tears To The Eye
Your Innocence Is Precious
Your Smile Is Pure Gold
You Are My Shining Light
I Long To Hold You Close
I Treasure Every Moment
Miss You When You're Gone
You Will Always Be My Angel
Who Could Never Do No Wrong
Now Your Little Brother
Has Joined Us In The World
I Am The Luckiest Grandma
In The Universe
Life Is Complete
Babes So Sweet

Runaway Bride

My Darling Bride
What Did I Do?
No Other Could Love You More!
I Gave You My Heart
Gave You My Soul
Still You Choose To Run!
Why Not Confide?
How Could You Lie?
Waited Until The Last!
Church Full Of People
Family And Friends
How Could You Do This?
Alas...
I Could Give You The World
Name But Your Price
Material Things Don't Entice
Was It Nerves?
Did You Panic?
You Have Left Me Bereft!
Please Come Back To Me...
I Will Never Give Up On You
You Are Blind
Open Your Eyes And See!

Row Your Boat

Row Row Row Your Boat
Over The Rippled Lake
The Scent Of Spring Is In The Air
Pink Blossom Sweet
Romance Of The Hopeful
Bold And Carefree
The Little Boat Glides With Ease
Cool To The Touch
The Water Below
The Dusk Of The Day
Doth Creep
Nocturnal Life Awakens
Mystically Unique
The Lapping Sound Of Gentle Waves
Curl Around The Boat
The Sunset On The Horizon
Makes For A Scenic Burst
A Perfect Landscape Painting
The Scene Would Surely Make
So Row On Little Boat
Row On
Gliding Proud And Free
Nowhere Else Would I Be

Déjà Vu

I Know That I Have Had
This Memory Before
Not Sure How
Not Sure When
But *Certain*

My Mind It Tries To Trick Me
Yet I *Have* Been Here
Somehow...
It Stops Me For A Moment
The Familiarity

The Phenomenon Is Haunting
A Sensation That Is Strong
The Recollection Imminent
This Feeling
Strange...

It Is Like A Name
On The Tip Of One's Tongue
It *Is* There
But Not Quite-
Frustrating...

This Sudden Recognition
With A Fancy French Name
Has Happened To Me Several Times
It Is Most Bizarre
I Can Not Explain
This Déjà Vu

Alaska

'Alaska'
Unpolished...
Beautiful To Me
The Whitest Glaciers
Raw-
My Breath Doth Catch
Oh My Greedy Eyes
Fat And Full
The Scene Devoured-
Giant Grizzly
In His Prime
Magnificent
Free...
Rugged
Notorious
Unforgiving Place
Keeper Of A Thousand Secrets-
Late September I Come
When The Northern Lights Appear
There Is Something
Eerie
Chilling
It Has Become My Drug
Draws Me In
Keeps Me Close
My Heart It Doth Belong Here...
Nature At Its Finest
The Land That Time Forgot
A Little Piece Of Heaven
My Blanket Most Secure
My Happy Ever After
Past
Present
And Future-

Happy Feet

Passion Of A Tango
Beating Of One's Heart
Sets The Soul On Fire
Gives The Biggest Spark

Finesse Of The Foxtrot
Smooth Flowing Moves
Elegance Unchallenged
Floating Soft And True

Performed In Closed Position
Gliding Across The Floor
So Close We're Almost Touching
Waltz I Most Adore

Along Came Lively Rock And Roll
Athletic From The Start
Gets The Blood Flow Pumping
Its Funk Sets It Apart

Smoking Rumba Hot And Wild
Swaying Of The Hips
Body Action Overtime
Authentic And Quick

The Jolly Little Quickstep
Flicks And Hops And Skips
Very Energetic
Sure To Keep You Fit

Into The Deep

Beneath The Ocean
Vast And Dark
The Secrets Of The Deep
Species Undiscovered
Unnamed Unique-
A Hidden World
Locked Away
Since The Dawn Of Time
An Alien Existence
Unseen By Modern Man-
Sunken Ships
Lay Scattered
Upon The Ocean Floor
Once Were Such A Splendour
Now That Is No More-
This Place Is Unforgiving
A Hard Nut To Crack
A Very Different Rhythm
So Relaxed-
The Weird And The Wonderful
Coexist As One
Elaborate Formation
Warmer Shores-
The Coral Reef
Colourful
Bursting Forth With Life
An Ecosystem
Carbonates
Invigorating
Sight-
The Mystery
The Questions
Deepest Blue Shore

Land Of Make Believe

Fairy Dust And Toadstools
A World Of Make Believe
A Childs Imagination
Spotty Flying Pigs...

Peter Pan Most Dashing
Leader Of The Lost
Captain Hook Most Deadly
Crocodile Tick Tock

Clouded Breath Most Icy
Jack Nipping At Your Nose
In The Midst Of Winter
Barren Like The Rose

Talking Elves And Pixies
Living Up In Space
Floating Through The Hemisphere
World A Better Place

Fire Breathing Dragons
Dwell Under The Bed
Sugar Plum Fairies
Dance Around One's Head

Climb Aboard This Cardboard Box
Sail The Seven Seas
Avoiding The Pirate Clan
Back Home For Tea

Fallen Angels

They Walk Among Us Hand In Hand
A Silence Unspoken
Retracted Wings Cast Aside
Stripped Bare
Naked-
Their Holy Wrath Untamed
Uncaptured Can't Contain
'Tis God Has Another Plan
Pasture Is Short
Cloaked Under A Thickened Sheath
The Call Is Unexplained
Vacant...
A Faceless Angel Has No Name
Forgotten To The Cause
Society Does Not See
Blinded-
Oh Blessed Fallen Angel
Contrite Heart
Protector Of Mankind
Compassionate Celestial
With The Ability To Smite-
Open Wide Your Loving Arms
Watch Over The Meek
Divine Intervention
A Common Misbelief-
Like A Shower From Above
Angels Are Falling
Tonight

The Sky At Night

Captivating Creamy Mix
Astronomer Delight
Dazzling Orion Of Nebula
Clouds Of Gas And Dust
Thirteen Thousand Light Years
A Winter Sighting First-
The Springly Constellations
Draco Cygnus And Lyra
The Kepler Space Telescope
Keeps A Watchful Eye-
Possibilities Are Infinite
Discovering New Things
The Thickened Mass
Of Brightest Stars
Set Against The Night-
The Perseids In August
A Meteor Display
Grace Us With Their Presence
Come What May-
Jupiter In Virgo
Brightest From The South
Arcturus In The East
Shining Loud And Proud-
Comets Through Binoculars
Waxed Crescent Moon
Fresh And Pure
Majestic
Come Back Soon

Reaper

Hello Again My Faithful Friend
'Tis Silent Tears You Cry
The Bloodied Wounds Are Open
I Need To Say Goodbye

We Met Upon The Battlefield
On A Cold November Day
The First Time That You Came For Me
Alas I Would Not Lay

Another Time A Different Place
The Battle We Have Lost
Fallen Friends And Comrades
Have Taken Up Their Posts

I Drink It In The Sights And Smells
Feel Sunlight On My Skin
Drunk With Elation
New Era To Begin

My Eyes Are Wide And Heavy
My Body Ebbs Away
Drifting Off Peacefully
Soul Doth Slip Away

Unconscious

Floating High
Floating Free
This Feeling
Make It Last...
I Beg Of You
A Thousand Eyes
A Thousand Ears
Have Dreamt This Dream Before
Each One Yearning
Preservation-
A Stalemate
The Greying Steel
Hard
Cold To The Touch
Yet I Hold The Blade?
Muddied With Blood
Remove This Parasite From Within
Extraction-
Take Me Back
I Beg Of Thee
For The Nightmare Is Dark
Unbearable-
Let Me Feel Again
Let Me Taste
Essence Of Life
Bursting Heart
Happiness Devoured
Lighter Than The Bee
Weightless...
Reptilic Like The Snake
Shedding Skin
Reborn
I Want This
Take Me There...

Roll Up Roll Up

It Came When The World Was Sleeping
Pitched Up Within A Field
The Thrills Of The Big Top
Are Priceless-
Not Sure When
Unsure How
By Noon A Gathered Crowd
Word Of Mouth Has Got Around
The Secret Is Now Out-
Flying High Trapeziums
Danger Wall Of Death
Funny Clowns
Acrobats
The Circus Is The Best-
Spillage Of One's Popcorn
For Thrills That Do Surprise
Hotdogs And Candy Canes
Flashing Hand Held Lights-
It Is Magical
It Is Awesome
And Children Love It Too
If Only I Was Young Again
I Would Run Away With You

A Squirrel's Song

Where Are My Nuts?
I Left Them Just There
My Neighbour Has Pinched Them
Well I Declare!
It Took Me Forever
To Gather Them All
I'm Hopping Mad
I'm Standing Tall
Why Oh Why
Did I Leave My Nuts
It Was Just For A Moment
That's All It Took
Daylight Is Fading
I've Nothing To Show
Supper Is Cancelled
It's Such A Blow
Oh How I Miss You
My Big Juicy Pile
I *Will* Get You Back
It May Take A While
Never Again
Would I Leave Thee
Out In The Open
For The World To See

Ode Of The Smitten

What Is This I'm Feeling
A Different Way To Be
Mellow As The Summer Sky
Floating Clouds I See

A Flutter In The Tummy
Happy All Day Long
Blowing Leaves Upon The Breeze
The Blackbird's Chirpy Song

I Think Of You When I Wake Up
Until The Silver Moon
The Spell You Cast Upon Me
Creates A Playful Tune

I Would Marry You Tomorrow
In Sickness And In Health
For Richer Or Poorer
Sweeping With My Stealth

The Hand Of Fate Astounds Me
Fitting Like A Glove
I Never Thought It Possible
To Be In Love

A Parody Of Summer

The Birdsong In The Meadow
A Floating Lily Pond
Cascading Weeping Willow
Pinkest Blossom Shrub
Playful Otters Peeping
Fishermen That Snooze
Scattered Seeds That Anchor
Blown In Lightest Breeze
Dragon Fly Who Hovers
Searching For His Food
Water Vole Doth Scurry
Golden Honey Bee
Frogs In Copulation
Love Is In The Air
Sweetest Buds And Pearly Shoots
New Life Everywhere
Soak It In
Like A Sponge
Spores Within My Chest
Wash Away Those Winter Blues
Summer Song Abreast
A Sheen Upon The Water
Reflective Rippled Hue
Warming Rays Of Golden Sun
Toes That Dip To Cool

Singing In The Rain

Splattered Splodge Of Muddied Boots
Rain Does Not Relent
Yet There Is Something Melancholy
Calm-
Thickest Mud
Squelch Doth Sound
Crunch Of Gravel
Gritty
Leaves Bow Under The Weight
By Raindrops From Above-
Pitter Patter On Fabric Loud
The Raincoat Does Its Job
Dog Unawares
Fur Matted And Wet
Darting Through The Undergrowth
Faithful Doting Pet-
Swollen River Has Burst Its Banks
A Months Droplets In A Day
Barren Fields
Oh Ruined Crop
The Power Of The Rain-
Huddled Birds
Cold And Soaked
Wait For This To Pass
I Sing In Jubilation
Notes Louder Than The Last

Hail Caesar

Hail Caesar They Say
The Great Roman Rule
Fifteen Years He Led Strong
Especially In Gaul

Oh The Battle Of Pompeii
Political Control
Many Looked Up To Him
The Dictator Of Rome

With Much Success Comes Jealousy
The Green Eyed Monster Waits
Hidden In The Shadows
Enemy Of The State

In The Year 46BC
His Victory Short Lived
His Assassination Plotted
By Marcus Junius Brutus

'Twere His Former Friend And Ally
Betrayed Him In The End
The Idles Of March Created
When Caesar's Rule Had Spent

Hail Caesar We Remember
History Is Wrote
Greatest Roman Ruler
Fiery Anecdote

Let There Be Hope

What Is The Soul Without Hope?
Broken And Dark...
Hope *Is* That Glint Of Light
Peeping Through The Cracks
Elevating Spirits
Giving Strength
Spreading Like A Branch
It Only Takes The Smallest Seed
The Magnificent Will Flourish-
I Compare Thee
To The Whitest Water Rapid
Crazy And Wild
Uncontrollable...
Emotions Spun Dry
Surplus To Requirements-
'Tis Like The Chink In One's Armoury
I Yearn For That
Alas I Yearn...
Rip Away The Sticky
Let The Spirit Heal
Harness All The Good
Take Hold With Both Hands
Never Let Go
White Knuckled Grasp
Immune

Fated

Romeo And Juliet
Two Lovers In Divide
Forbidden Like The Apple
Of Which Eve Took The Bite

Tragedy Forsakes Them
Romeo Thinks Thee Dead
Sips The Blackest Poison
The Hand Of Fate Mislead

Cleopatra And Mark Anthony
Deepest Darkest End
Defeated By The Romans
Suicide Transcends

Broken Hearted Lovers
Sparse Like Barren Field
Sorrow Doth Entangle
Happiness Concealed

Lancelot And Guinevere
Napoleon Josephine
Shah Jahan And Mumtaz Mahal
Unpicked At The Seams

Hand Was Dealt Unbreakable
Black Rain Upon The Wind
Clouded Cloak Befitting
Romantic Notions Thinned

Woe Is Painful Silence
Breaking Heart Bled
Undistinguished Embers
Unity Is Dead

Perception

I Am Blind But Yet I See
Steel So Cold
Warmest Heart
Silence Speaks A Thousand Tongues
Enlighten Me!
Ancient Language
Lost In Time
Smeared On Painted Caves
A Different Civilisation
Another Time
A Different Place-
The Mind It Tricks The Conscience
Mirage Within The Heat
Soothing Like An Ointment
Drifting Like The Breeze-
A Kindled Fire
Within The Crust
Molten Lava Stirs
Can Melt Away A Hundred Sins
Purifying Earth-
Shattered Dreams Like Porcelain
Crumbled Into Dust
Sifted Through The Fingers
Caught Upon The Breeze…
Savaged Arid Landscape
Ravaged By The Sun
Bathed In Tranquility
Midnight Moon

Shipwrecked

Fierce Storm Has Cast Me Out
Wrecked Upon Black Mittens
The Sea Is Unrelentless
Unforgiven

A Splurge Of Preservation
Washed Up Upon The Shore
Strange New Land Discovered
Soon To Be Explored

At First I Did Not Worry
I Knew That They Would Come
In Search Of Their Commander
Through The Summer Sun

That Was Once Upon A Time
With Hope Within My Heart
Now With Many Moons That Pass
I Do Not Feel As Smart

Why Do They Not Find Me?
My Ribs Could Play A Tune
My Beard Has Grown Thick And Long
Neath This Silver Moon

Grandma's Apple Pie

Running Through The Blossom Field
On A Summer Afternoon
Beaming Lips Skipping Heart
Sun Upon My Face

The Delicious Smell Of Grandma
Carried On The Wind
Sweet Apple Pie Most Homely
Traditional And Unique

Ripened Apple Crisp And Sweet
Picked From Orchard Fair
Succulent Piece Of Heaven
Tender Loving Care

My Favourite Childhood Memory
Of An Era Passed
Closing My Eyes Tightly
The Thought Of Which Will Last

The Crumbled Melted Pastry
Bathed In Cream
Topped With Brambly Deep
A Small Child's Dream

Nothing Compares To You
Aroma Sweet And Scrummy
Dreamy Fulfilling
Get In My Tummy!

Jolly Roger

A Pirate's Life Upon The Sea
Scurvy At Its Best
Ships Rats Are A Plenty
Like Rum On Bated Breath
Pirate Gold To Die For
Some Will Walk The Plank
Fierce Are The Scavengers
Many Boats They Sank
Come Sail Away
Come Sail Away
Come Sail Away With Me
The Tide A Bonnie Lassie
On The Lashing Sea
Yo Ho Ho
A Bottle Of Rum
'Tis The Familiar Cry
Docked Upon The Harbour
With Evil In The Eye
Come Sail Away
Come Sail Away
Come Sail Away With Me
The Tide A Bonnie Lassie
On The Lashing Sea

Optical Illusions

Wisp Of Cloud Across The Moon
Cascading Waterfall
Trickled Splash Upon The Rock
Flawless…
Milky Gem Of Sweet Delight
Reddened Sky At Night
Crystal Clear Waters
Tranquility…
Blue Grass Field
Cotton Tails
Water Lily White
Bewitching…
Minky Fur
Satin Sheen
Aromatic Scent
Sweet…
Ashen Bark
Blossom Peach
Softest Sumptuous Silk
Exquisite…
Sprightly Lambs In Bluebell Fields
Prancing In The Sun
Unfolding Buds That Open
Delicate…
Speckled Frog
Golden Ponds
Ripples Reaching Forth
Symmetrical…
Painted Like The Lady
Fluttering On The Breeze
Graceful And Alluring
Angelic…
Luscious Grass
Mellowed
Calming
Captivating…

The Witching Hour

One Minute Past Three
The Strange Begins
Bewitching Hour Is Here
Monsters And Ghouls
Come Out To Play
Shivering Spines Of Fear
The Closet Creep
The Weird Doth Reign
Blood Eyes Bore Deepest Soul
Electrifying Static Feel
Fullest Whole Blue Moon
Bite Of Werewolf
Witches Spell
Frogs And Toads Immune
Spider's Web Toe Of Newt
Stirred With Giant's Drool
Something Special Happens Here
Silence As Time Stands Still
A Devil's Curse Is Born Again
Daring Like The Wind
The Dead Awaken In Their Graves
Break Through Fertile Soil
Lurching Through The Misty Haze
Looking For Fresh Blood

Take Me To Church

Take Me To Church
The Gospel Choir
Keep Singing
Oh Keep Singing-
Hallowed Name
My Prayer Of Faith
Save Me
Oh Save Me-
Damnation Aside
The Demon Is Out
Banish Him
Oh Banish Him-
Child Of Innocence
Baptised In Light
Embrace Them
Oh Embrace Them-
Give Us This Day
Our Daily Bread
Sustain Me
Oh Sustain Me-
Sacred Vows
Of Binding Souls
Join Them
Oh Join Them-
Forgive Us Now
Our Wicked Sins
Repent Them
Oh Repent Them-
Cleanse The Body
Free The Mind
Guide Us
Oh Guide Us-
Holy Spirit
Pure Divinity
Enlighten
Oh Enlighten-

Enlightenment

Royal Lagoon Come Drink Me Up
Immerse Into Your Cool
Hidden Pockets Under Wash
Secrets Are Discovered
Hold Your Breath A Thousand Times
Greedy Eyes Demand It!
A Strange New World
Almost Alien
Feeling Foreign-
A Glint Reflective
Sparkled Shawls
Darting To And Fro
Elusive-
Come Let Us Dive
Deeper Still
As We Unlock The New
Creature Comforts Disappear
The Hideous Undone
Prickle Stings Like Aftershock
Beauty Is Bereft
Yet We Grow To Love This Thing
Even Its Ugliness-
Fame And Fortune
Seek The Meek
A New Species Found
Media Is In A Spin
With That It's Homeward Bound

Capturing Canada

Misty Fog On Hardened Scape
Icy Breeze Doth Blow
Snow Capped Earth
A Wilderness
Wild And White Reserve-
Ashen Bark On Knotted Tree
Sheltered Silver Dunes
Wonderland Of Savages
Under Starry Moon-
Sense Of Sound Becomes Alert
Howl Of Wolf Is Carried
Blowing Through The Valley Peaks
Weary And Unhurried-
Nipping Cold On Fingers Bare
Carbon Smoky Breath
Crackled Orbs Like Chandeliers
Melt In Lighter Air-
Volcanic Stream
On Mountain Glen
Trickled Fresh And Pure
The Source Of Life To Many
Dispelling Thirst For Sure-
Rolling In
Sheets Of Sleet
Cloaked Clouds
Masquerade
Covering Correctiveness
Alpine
Darkened
Shade

The Ark

Into The Ark
Quickly Now
The First Rain Has Begun
Darkened Sky
Thickest Clouds
Angry...
The Speckled Spots
Soon Turn Wild
Ravishing Their Cleanse
Wash Away
Man Made Sin
Purify The Land...
Into The Ark
Two By Two
Survival Of The Species
Taken Forth
Flooded Shores
Grasping To Existence...
Waves Rage High
Fifty Feet
Swollen Power Swells
Clouds Are Unrelentless
Pouring Forth Their Wealth...
Greying Sky Surrounding
Ransoming Their Loot
Cloaked Within The Fortress
Discovering The Truth...
Cast Out The Evil
Forgive Us For Our Sins
Let Us Live In Harmony
Preservation Wins

Birdsong

I Will Follow Thee
In Meadow Blue
Azure
Sapphire
Cyan
The Bluebell Scent
In The Air
Divine-
The Warming Sun
Upon Me Shine
Makes Thee Sing Again
Angelic
Like An Angel's Wing
I Love The Tune You Bring…
Sweetest Music
Do Not Stop
Sing Little Songbird Sing
Fill Me With Your Spirit
Make Me Whole Again-
I Find You In The Graveyard
I Find You Through The Glen
I Find You In This Meadow
Sing For Me Again…
I Would Follow You Forever
To Eternity And A Day
Wrapped Within Your Melodies
Where I Want To Stay

Sweet Tooth

Caramel Poured
Sweet And Light
Whipped Cream
Fluffed Up Peaks
Blind Baked Flan
Homemade Cakes
Chocolate Orange Treats-
Touch Of Spice
Rolled Cinnamon
Bread And Putter Pud
Soft Sultanas Melting
Sorbet Very Good-
Dusted Tops Of Icing Sugar
Looks Like Sifted Snow
Fruit Filled Pies
Blackcurrant Jam
Golden Crunchy Dough-
Macaroon Of Coconut
Melting On The Tongue
Lemon Cheesecake
Crunchy Base
Topping Big And Bold-
Sugar Donuts
Light And Round
Fresh Cream Scones
Crumble Browned
Crispy Cakes
Ice Cream Rounds-
Yes I Am A Pudding Gal
With A Girth To Match
Fun Loving Chocolatier
Certainly A Catch…

Missing In Action

You've Been Gone A While
Oh My Dearest Hal
Alas Many Moons Hath Passed
You Left To Serve Your Country Men
Fields Of Poppy Now Grass

The Bombs They Do Drop
And I Pray To God
For Your Safe Return
Only Married For A Month
I Seek Your Loving Arms

The Air Raid Shelters
Are Packed To Burst
This War Is So Unfair
Please Return I Shed My Tears
For Your Loss I Could Not Bear

My Legs They Did Buckle
The Day That It Came
That Telegram Of Doom
Missing It Action It Declared
Unlikely To Resume

The Life Of Henry The VIII

Henry The Eighth
He Married Six Times
A Tudor King
Through And Through
Famous For His Rounded Girth
And The Enemies That He Slew

Renouncing From The Catholic Church
In Fifteen Thirty Three
He Founded A New Religion
The Church Of England
Was To Be

Two Of His Wives
Anne Boleyn And Kathryn Howard
Met A Sticky End
Executed By Their Spouse
Off With Their Heads

At The Age Of Fifty Six
Henry Came To Pass
Succeeded By Edward VI
The Reign Of Who Was Short
Elizabeth I Did Rule Many Moons To Come

Broken

Beating Heart A Thousand Scars
Bleeding Vein Of Truth
Locked Away Deep Within
Unseeing…

Papered Seal Cracked And Torn
Withered Like The Flower
A Reaper's Hand Has Cursed The Soul
Unyielding…

Let It Grow That Seed Of Doubt
Encasing Like The Vine
Suffocating Toxic Thoughts
Relentless…

Blinded Eyes That Cannot See
Humanities Are Lost
Tainted Senses Lost To Thee
Darkness…

Cast Forth Your Spell You Wicked Witch
Heart Made Out Of Stone
Wing Of Bat And Tongue Of Frog
Atonement…

Cutting Deep The Twisted Thorn
Etched Into The Skin
Driven Ever Deeper
Damnation…

Unique

Relentless Rain Resourceful
Scorched Sahara Sun
Abominable Antarctic
Frozen-
Budding Blossom Blowing
Floating Feathers Fresh
Midnight Moon Magnificent
Astounding-
Ruby Robin Redbreast
Perched Perfection Preened
Beautiful Bewitching
Priceless-
Dusty Daydreams Dancing
High Above The Hills
Calming Cosmic Celestial
Healing-
Warming Whispered Welcome
Shining Starry Skies
Emerald Encasing
Dazzling-
This World Is Amazing
The Little Things I See
Unnoticeable To Others
But Not To Me...
I See This Wondrous Planet
The Secrets That It Holds
I Worship Every Second
The Sunshine And The Cold...
The Reddened Leaves Go Crispy
They Crunch Beneath Your Feet
Seasons Are Changing
Perfection

Letting Go

Will You Stay With Me
When The Time Arrives?
Don't Want To Be Alone
Alas My Final Journey
Beckons Very Soon-
I Have Lived The Fullest Life
Travelled Far And Wide
Met Amazing People
Fills Me With Much Pride-
I Remember When I Saw You
Across The Cobbled Street
Looking Very Handsome
My Eyes Got Quite A Treat-
I Loved You Then
I Love You Now
More Than You Could Know
You Have Been My Life
My Darling
Oh How I Love You So
I Really Have To Go Now
My Love
Please Don't Cry
Goodbye...

Cheating Heart

I Saw You Today
I Know What You Did
You Thought You Were
Home And Dry
But The Eyes
They Can See You
Watching Forever
Not Happy Ever After Am I
Why Did You Do This?
What Pushed You So
I Thought We Were
Stronger Than This
Don't Try To Deny It
I Am Not Going Mad
My Darling
You Have Lost Me For This
The Vows You Have Broken
Without A Care
My Heart It Is Now Ripped In Two
The Pain It May Fade
I Am Sure In Time
Goodbye…
I Deserve Someone Better Than You!

Under The Weather

Swollen Glands
Reddened Eyes
Gastric Flu
Coughs And Colds
A Temperature
Get Me To The Loo-
Broken Bones
Stubbed Fat Toes
Bandages Galore
Runny Nose
Flaky Skin
Feeling Very Sore-
Water Infection
Chapped Lips
Diarrhoea
Lumps And Bumps
Spotty Pox
Itchy Middle Ear-
Haemorrhoids
Jaundice
Slipped Lower Disc
Sticky Eyes
Extra Hives
I Feel Sick-
Cut Knees
Twisted Ankle
Big Fat Lip
Conjunctivitis
Skin Caught In A Zip-
Bitten By A Rattlesnake
Stung By A Bee
Fetch The Anti-Venom
Tragedy-
Quick Call A Doctor
Holler For The Nurse
Get Me To The Hospital
Before It Gets Worse!

The Two Faces Of Nature

Hostile Planet
Ravaged Dreams
Winds Have Stripped It Bare
Thirsty Earth
Split-
Scorched By Heat
Fiery Sun
Rains Have Yet To Come
Withered Crop
Faded-
The Wilderness
Seeking Shade
Desperate To Survive
Waiting For The Cool Of Dusk
Hunt Before First Light-
Arid Desert
Sand So Hot
Arabian Nights
So Smooth
Meandering Mirage
Wet-
Go Drink It In
Soak It Up
Clouds Are Full And Round
Unleashing Their Contents
Where Devastation Is Found-
Yet Again Replenished
Nature At Its Best
Cracked Baked Ground
Softened
Swollen Rivers Blessed-
How The Gods
Have Spoken
The Damned
Reprieved

Stand And Deliver

Oh Highwayman
Upon Your Steed
Waiting In The Shadows
The Gentry
Richest Pickings
Yours For The Taking-
Stand And Deliver
Your Money Is Undone
Possessions Are Omitted
Once Staring At The Gun-
'Tis A Dangerous Living
They Catch You
You Are Hung
An Outlaw
Who Is Feared
When All Is Said And Done-
Give To Him Your Treasures
Your Money
For You Life
Turn Away Your Hero
It Brings A World Of Strife-
Dashing Is The Villain
Dressed In Finest Cloth
Danger Quite Appealing
Ladies Who Will Blush-
Battle Scars
Sated Wound
The Wealthy Lords
Fullest Moon

Once Upon A Dream

It Is The Moments
Before I Awake
My Reoccurring Dream
Vivid Like It Was Yesterday
Oh What Can It Mean-
I Remember Walking
Through The Sea
Parted By My Hands
The Sea Turtles
Who Swim Aside
Wet And Cooling Sand-
Mermaids Surround
Their Longest Locks
Blowing Fine And Free
They Wave To Me
From Yonder Rocks
I Rub My Eyes To see-
I Walk Across The Ocean
Intrigued By What I Find
An Oyster's Pearl
My Treasured Loot
In Light Of Truth I'm Bound-
Discovering Long Lost Kingdoms
Atlantis I Have Found
A Derelict Desertion
Hidden-

Have You Ever?

Have You Ever Seen A Ghost
In The Dead Of Night?
Do You Thrive On Horror Films
Chills Running Down Your Spine?

Have You Ever Loved And Lost
A Thousand Or Times Or More?
Broken Heart That Heals In Time
Harder Than Before

Have You Ever Cried And Cried
Your Tears Could Fill A River?
Have You Ever Almost Died
Cheating Death's Grey Reaper?

Have You Ever Gazed Upon
The Whitest Stars At Night?
Twinkling Their Merriment
Shining Very Bright

Have You Ever Laughed So Hard
Your Sides Begin To Ache?
Smiling Eyes And Faces
Heartwarming Embrace

Haunted

Deep Within The Dark Dark Woods
There Lies A Chilling Sight
The Ghost Of A Grey Lady
Who Walks Around At Night

Clothed In Late Victorian
A Bonnet On Her Head
She Scares The Living Daylights
Out Of Anyone Who Treads

Come The Dead Can't Hurt You
It's The Living You Must Fear
There's Nothing To Be Scared Of
So Let Go Of My Ear

Can You Feel The Coldness
A Ghost Has Touched Your Soul
Please Stop Your Screaming
Or Deaf I Just May Go

Leave Me Here
Just Go Home
It's On With The Hunt
All Alone

My Jamie

Most Days
You Will Hear Me Say
'Jamie Get Down From There!'
He Jumps Upon The Sofa
Without The Slightest Care
Yesterday He Fell Hard
The Tears They Did Flow
But Only Moments Later
He Was Having Another Go
My Face Is Always Peachy
Scrunched Up As I Yell
But Jamie Will Be Jamie
And He's At It Yet Again!
He Tries To Cosplay Superman
He Thinks That He Can Float
I Screech
'Jamie'
'You're Not A Mountain Goat!'
My Furniture Is Ruined
My Voice Is Hoarse
The Joys Of Having Jamie
My Nerves Are Shot Of Course

It's A Boy Thing

My Pockets Are Full
Stuffed With Worms
From Garden They Did Come
Muddy Pies
And Lots Of Flies
I'm Stig Of This Dump-
My Brother
He Is Mean To Me
He Punched Me In The Arm
He Tied Me To The Lamp Post
But I Came To No Harm-
I Built A Den Within A Day
Magnificent It Was
Until It Rained Cats And Dogs
It Is Now A Soggy Bog-
My Sister's Friend Is Goofy
She Has Lost Her Two Front Teeth
She Always Tries To Kiss Me
So I Have To Run At Speed…

Thank you for reading my collection of 100 word poems. I have included a diverse selection and each poem is different, with its own style. I have dedicated this book to my son Jamie, as he became so involved with the selection process. He was allowed to choose three poems for this book. After careful deliberation he chose A Squirrel's Song (which he found hilarious), The Noise and of course My Jamie.

My inspiration comes from personal experiences and the beautiful world around us.

www.ingramcontent.com/pod-product-compliance
Lightning Source LLC
Chambersburg PA
CBHW030332080526
44584CB00012B/825